Severe Weather

Heat Waves

by Trudy Becker

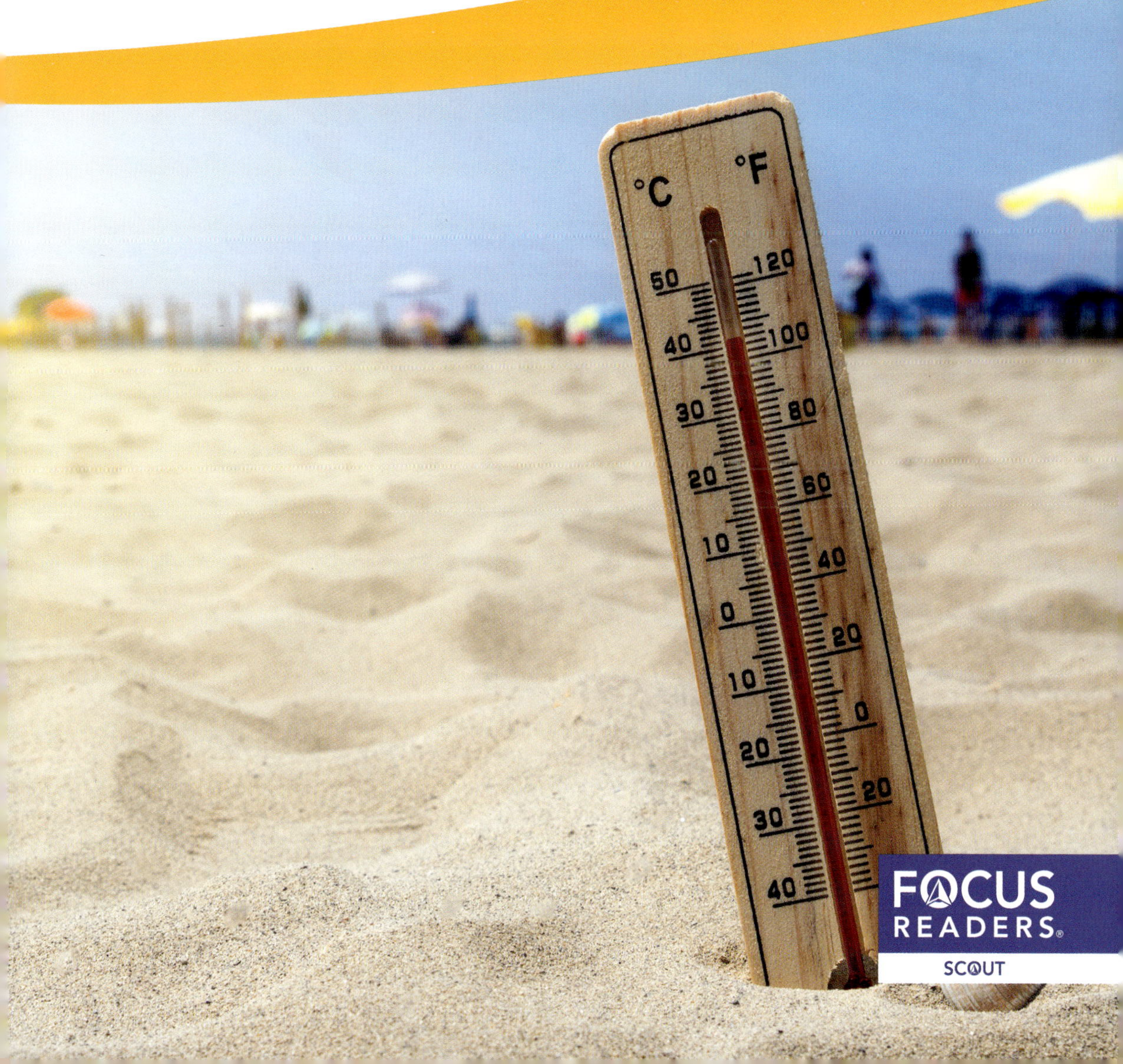

FOCUS READERS®
SCOUT

www.focusreaders.com

Focus Readers is distributed by North Star Editions:
sales@northstareditions.com | 888-417-0195

Produced for Focus Readers by Red Line Editorial.

Photographs ©: iStockphoto, cover, 1, 4, 8, 11, 12, 15 (top), 16 (top left), 16 (bottom left); Shutterstock Images, 7, 15 (bottom), 16 (top right), 16 (bottom right)

Library of Congress Cataloging-in-Publication Data
Names: Becker, Trudy author
Title: Heat waves / Trudy Becker.
Description: Mendota Heights, MN: Focus Readers, [2026] | Series: Severe weather | Includes index. | Audience: Grades K-1
Identifiers: LCCN 2025022906 (print) | LCCN 2025022907 (ebook) | ISBN 9798889986270 hardcover | ISBN 9798889986348 paperback | ISBN 9798889986478 pdf | ISBN 9798889986416 ebook
Subjects: LCSH: Heat waves (Meteorology)--Juvenile literature
Classification: LCC QC981.8.A5 B43 2026 (print) | LCC QC981.8.A5 (ebook) | DDC 551.5/253--dc23/eng/20250818
LC record available at https://lccn.loc.gov/2025022906
LC ebook record available at https://lccn.loc.gov/2025022907

Printed in the United States of America
Mankato, MN
012026

About the Author

Trudy Becker lives in Minneapolis, Minnesota.

Table of Contents

What Are Heat Waves?

The air is hot.

The ground is hot.

The heat does not go away.

No clouds form.

No rain falls.

The heat is not safe.

It is a heat wave.

Country and City

Heat waves hit many places.

They hit in the **country**.

Plants get hot.

They dry out.

Heat waves hit in the **city**.

Buildings block wind.

Cars add heat.

Heat waves get worse.

Keep Safe

The sun shines down.

It burns skin.

People get too hot.

They feel sick.

Stay in the **shade**.

Drink water.

Use a **fan**.

Keep safe in heat waves!

fan

Glossary

city

fan

country

shade

Index